TEXAS

Janice Parker

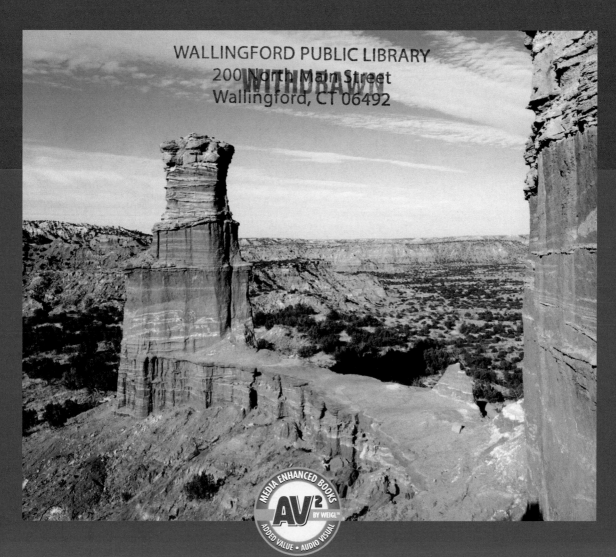

www.av2books.com

AV² provides enriched content that supplements and complements this book. Weigl's AV² books strive to create inspired learning and engage young minds in a total learning experience.

Your AV² Media Enhanced books come alive with...

Audio
Listen to sections of the book read aloud.

Key Words
Study vocabulary, and complete a matching word activity.

Video
Watch informative video clips.

Quizzes
Test your knowledge.

Embedded Weblinks
Gain additional information for research.

Slide Show
View images and captions, and prepare a presentation.

Try This!
Complete activities and hands-on experiments.

... and much, much more!

Go to **www.av2books.com**, and enter this book's unique code.

BOOK CODE

F379437

AV² by Weigl brings you media enhanced books that support active learning.

Published by AV² by Weigl
350 5th Avenue, 59th Floor
New York, NY 10118
Website: www.av2books.com

Library of Congress Cataloging-in-Publication Data
Names: Parker, Janice.
Title: Texas : the Lone Star State / Janice Parker.
Description: New York, NY : AV2 by Weigl, 2016. | Series: Discover America |
  Includes index.
Identifiers: LCCN 2015048059 (print) | LCCN 2015049103 (ebook) | ISBN
  9781489649478 (hard cover : alk. paper) | ISBN 9781489649485 (soft cover :
  alk. paper) | ISBN 9781489649492 (Multi-User eBook)
Subjects: LCSH: Texas--Juvenile literature.
Classification: LCC F386.3 .P354 2016 (print) | LCC F386.3 (ebook) | DDC 976.4--dc23
LC record available at http://lccn.loc.gov/2015048059

Printed in the United States of America, in Brainerd, Minnesota
1 2 3 4 5 6 7 8 9 20 19 18 17 16

082016
210715

Project Coordinator Heather Kissock
Art Director Terry Paulhus

Photo Credits
Every reasonable effort has been made to trace ownership and to obtain permission to reprint copyright material. The publisher would be pleased to have any errors or omissions brought to their attention so that they may be corrected in subsequent printings. The publisher acknowledges Getty Images, iStock Images, and Alamy as its primary image suppliers for this title.

TEXAS

Contents

AV² Book Code 2
Discover Texas 4

THE LAND
Beginnings 6
Where is Texas? 8
Land Features 10
Climate 12
Nature's Resources 14
Vegetation 16
Wildlife 18

ECONOMY
Tourism 20
Primary Industries 22
Goods and Services 24

HISTORY
Native Americans 26
Exploring the Land 28
The First Settlers 30
History Makers 32

CULTURE
The People Today 34
State Government 36
Celebrating Culture 38
Arts and Entertainment 40
Sports and Recreation 42

Get to Know Texas 44
Brain Teasers 46
Key Words/Index 47
Log on to www.av2books.com 48

STATE TREE
Pecan

STATE BIRD
Mockingbird

STATE MAMMAL (LARGE)
Texas Longhorn

STATE FLAG
Texas

STATE FLOWER
Bluebonnet

STATE SEAL
Texas

Nicknames
The Lone Star State

Song
"Texas, Our Texas,"
by William J. Marsh and
Gladys Yoakum Wright

Entered the Union
December 29, 1845, as the 28th state

Motto
Friendship

Population
(2010 Census) 25,145,561
Ranked 2nd state

Capital
Austin

Discover Texas

After Alaska, Texas is the largest state in area in the United States. For several years, this state was a nation of its own. It was called the **Republic** of Texas. That all changed on December 29, 1845, when Texas became the 28th state to join the Union.

Texas is as large as Kentucky, Ohio, Indiana, and all of the Middle Atlantic and New England states put together. Its various regions include mountains, forests, deserts, plains, and a subtropical coast. Few other states have such a wealth of mineral resources as Texas. In the twentieth century, Texas became the leading producer and refiner of oil in the United States.

The size and unique history of Texas have contributed to its culture. Ranchers, cattle herds, rodeos, and gushing oil wells all play an important part in Texas tradition. Although many people might imagine 10-gallon hats and cowboy boots when they think of Texas, there is much more to the state. For more than a century, Texas was part of Spain's North American empire, and for nearly 20 years, it was part of Mexico. Hispanic food, culture, and architecture all help to create a special atmosphere in the state.

Texas's nickname, the Lone Star State, comes from the state flag's one star on a blue strip. Beside it, a banner of white sits atop a banner of red. This flag was originally adopted in 1839 as the national flag of the Republic of Texas. After Texas joined the Union, it became the state flag. On the Texas flag, red stands for bravery, white stands for purity, and blue stands for loyalty.

The Land

Texas's Big Bend National Park is home to 1,200 different plant species, 450 bird species, and 56 types of reptiles.

Texas has a **367-mile coastline** on the Gulf of Mexico.

Under the terms of the 1845 resolution that made Texas a state, Texas has the right to **split into five separate states** at any time.

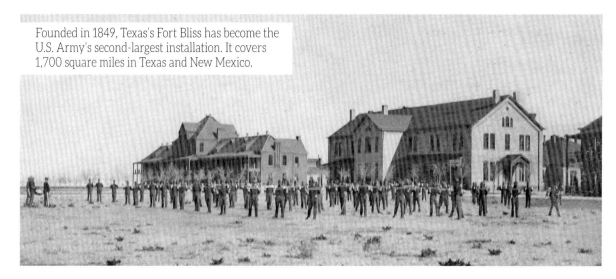

Founded in 1849, Texas's Fort Bliss has become the U.S. Army's second-largest installation. It covers 1,700 square miles in Texas and New Mexico.

Beginnings

Native Americans lived in Texas 10,000 to 12,000 years ago, and perhaps much earlier. By the beginning of the 1500s, dozens of Native American groups lived in the Texas area. The Caddo, an important Native American group in Texas, called themselves *thecas*. This name meant "friends" or "**allies**," because they banded together against Apache raiders. The Spanish spelled the word *tejas* or *texas* and used it to name the area where these people lived. The Apache and the Comanche arrived later from the north.

By the 1820s, when Mexico owned the land, settlers of European descent had developed a colony in the area that would be come Texas. In the 1830s, these settlers fought for independence against the Mexican government. The last battle of the war was fought in 1836, leading to peace negotiations. With the signing of the Treaties of Velasco, Texas was no longer held under Mexican rule.

After Texas gained independence, the initial population boom came from settlers attracted to the area's fertile soil. The two biggest immigrant groups were from the United States and Germany. Ranching and farming, particularly cotton, became even more important to the economy of Texas with the addition of the railroad in the 1870s. New towns popped up all along the railroad, attracting even more settlers interested in a variety of businesses.

Where is

TEXAS?

Texas sprawls across the south-central United States. The massive state spans 773 miles from its westernmost point to its easternmost locale, while 801 miles separate the northwest corner of the Texas **panhandle** and the southern tip of the state. The southeastern portion of Texas runs along the Gulf of Mexico, and the Rio Grande separates the state from the country of Mexico on the southwest.

MEXICO

2

United States Map

Alaska   Hawai'i

Texas

MAP LEGEND

- Texas
- ☆ Capital City
- Hueco Tanks State Historic Site
- ▲ The Fort Worth Stockyards
- Natural Bridge Caverns
- Bordering States
- Mexico
- River
- Water

1 Austin

Austin is in central Texas, on the north bank of the Colorado River. The community was originally called Waterloo. It was renamed in honor of Texas pioneer Stephen Austin in 1839, when it was chosen to be the capital of the recently formed Republic of Texas. Austin became the state capital when Texas joined the Union in 1845.

2 Hueco Tanks State Historic Site

Known for its world-class rock climbing, Hueco Tanks State Historic Site is just east of El Paso. Rock climbers who specialize in bouldering come from all over the world to experience this area's rock formations. Prehistoric people also left pictographs that visitors can experience.

OKLAHOMA

ARKANSAS

TEXAS

③

Austin ☆

①

LOUISIANA

④

Rio Grande

Gulf of Mexico

N

SCALE 0 ⸺ 125 miles

3 The Fort Worth Stockyards

The Stockyards National Historic District was founded in 1866. Millions of cattle were rested, sorted, or shipped out to other cities across Texas from this point. The stockyards are the last facilities of their kind. Today, visitors can experience rodeos, concerts, and western-themed shopping at the site.

4 Natural Bridge Caverns

Natural Bridge Caverns is a vast underground network of caves consisting of more than 10,000 different **stalactite** formations. King's Throne is a 40-foot wall of stalactites found in one of the largest caverns, known as the Castle of the White Giants.

Land Features

The four major land regions of Texas are the Gulf Coastal Plain in the south and east, the Central Lowland in the north, the Great Plains in the far north, central, and western parts of the state, and the Basin and Range Region in the far southwest. The Gulf Coastal Plain covers about two-fifths of the state. Running from the lower Rio Grande to the Louisiana border, it includes the bays and barrier islands of the coast as well as plains running about 150 miles inland. In the Great Plains, which includes the panhandle, only a few trees and shrubs grow among seas of short grasses. The **barren** Basin and Range Region includes mountains and high desert.

El Capitan

El Capitan, in Guadalupe Mountains National Park, is considered the most recognizable peak in the state. It is located near Texas's highest mountain, the 8,749-foot-tall Guadalupe Peak.

Big Bend National Park

This park is located in a remote area of southwestern Texas along the Rio Grande. The unique desert region includes mountains, canyons, arid landscapes, and many types of plants and animals.

Padre Island National Seashore

This site, located near Corpus Christi in southern Texas, stretches 113 miles along the state's Gulf Coast. The protected area features white-sand beaches and dunes, grasslands, and marshes that serve as home to a variety of wildlife.

Caddo Lake

Caddo Lake in northeastern Texas abounds with bald cypress trees and a variety of aquatic plants. It was the only natural lake in the state before it was dammed in the early 1900s.

Climate

Much of the state of Texas has warm, humid summers and cool winters. Along the coast, the weather stays mild throughout the year. The western highlands have dry, warm days and cold nights. Hurricanes can blow onshore from the Gulf of Mexico, and tornadoes touch down in north Texas every spring.

The warmest part of the state is the lower Rio Grande Valley. Average summer temperatures of 85° Fahrenheit and average winter temperatures of 60°F make it enjoyable year round. The coolest area is the windy panhandle, where summers average 79°F and winters average 35°F.

Average Annual Precipitation Across Texas

Yearly precipitation can vary greatly in Texas depending on location. What are some of the reasons why rainfall levels are so different around the state?

LEGEND

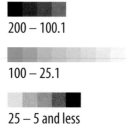

Average Annual Precipitation (in inches) 1961–1990

200 – 100.1

100 – 25.1

25 – 5 and less

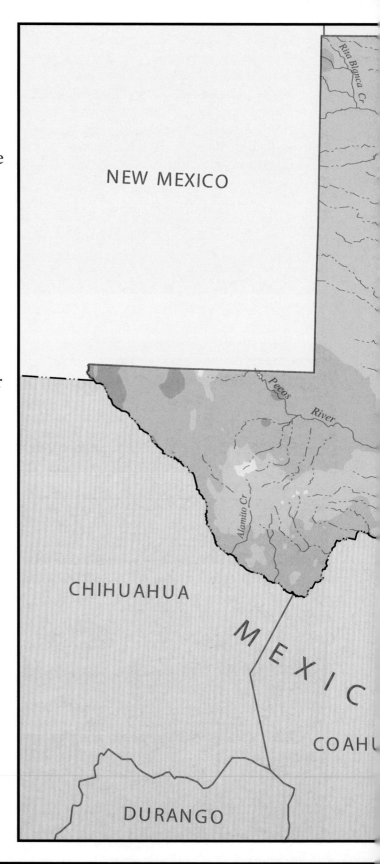

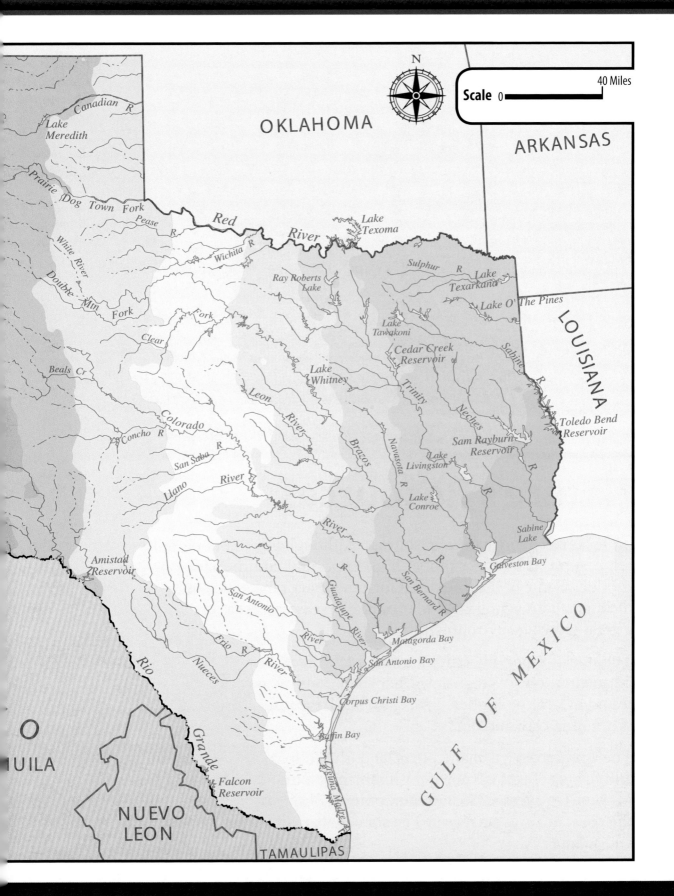

Oil deposits can found in more than two-thirds of the state's land area.

Nature's Resources

Texas has many natural resources. Although less than one-tenth of Texas is forested, timber is an important **commercial** product. Some of the trees used for timber are pine, oak, elm, hickory, and magnolia. Regular rainfall in eastern Texas creates a great growing environment.

The state is especially rich in mineral resources. Texas has more petroleum reserves than any other state. Natural gas and coal are found in large quantities. Texas also has large reserves of helium, salt, sulfur, clay, and talc.

The Texas coast has many **ports**, and is used for off-shore oil drilling and fishing. Texas is known for its shrimp, found in the Gulf of Mexico. On average, 56.5 million pounds of shrimp are caught off the coast of Texas each year. The state is also known for oysters and snapper.

Texas Gulf shrimp are special because they are wild caught. Most of the other shrimp eaten in the United States are from shrimp farms. Wild shrimp have created a food tourism industry along the Gulf Coast of Texas.

Texas is also the number-one wind energy producer in the U.S., providing the nation with one-third of its wind energy.

Vegetation

Texas is rich with fascinating plant life. The woodland areas of the state are home to pine and oak trees. Drier areas have mesquite, cactus, and sagebrush. The plains regions have hundreds of different types of grasses.

Thousands of plant species are native to Texas. Some 5,000 species of wildflowers bloom in the state. Bluebonnets, daisies, sunflowers, and asters are some of the most common flowers. The state plant of Texas is the prickly pear cactus. The fruit of the prickly pear is called tunas, and it makes delicious jelly. The flat pads, called nopales, are peeled and eaten as well. Grapefruits and many other citrus fruits are grown in Texas, although the plants are not native to the state.

Prickly Pear Cactus

The prickly pear is an edible variety of cactus most commonly found in the arid south and central Texas regions. Before the plant's fleshy pads can be eaten, its needles and hairlike spines must be removed. The prickly pear became the state plant in 1996.

Bluebonnets

The bluebonnet is a type of wildflower commonly seen growing along highways and rural roads in central and southern Texas. It blooms during the early spring. The bluebonnet was officially chosen as the state flower in 1971.

Mesquite Tree

The mesquite tree is one of the most widely found trees in Texas. It can grow to a height of 30 feet but often is much smaller. When burned, mesquite wood adds a pleasant flavor to foods and is popularly used in Texas-style barbecue.

Agave

The agave is a type of spiky plant found in the southern and western United States. There are many species of agave. A sweetener called agave nectar can be extracted from the plant. Agaves also are used to make the alcoholic beverage tequila.

Wildlife

Animal life abounds in Texas. The state has the most deer of any state in the nation. Jackrabbits, foxes, raccoons, pronghorns, and armadillos are other common Texas mammals. More than 100 species of snakes, including several poisonous types, live in Texas. The state also has many types of birds, including mockingbirds, hummingbirds, roadrunners, and prairie chickens.

Texas has several large bat colonies. At least 20 million bats live in Bracken Cave, near San Antonio. Every night, 1.5 million bats fly out from beneath the Congress Street Bridge in Austin.

Whooping cranes spend their winters in the Aransas National Wildlife Refuge. In the 1940s, there were fewer than 20 whooping cranes left in the world. **Conservation** workers bred the birds and released them into nature. Now there are more than 200 cranes living outside of captivity.

Armadillos

The armadillo is covered in plates of tough skin that serve as armor. The cat-sized mammal also has sharp claws that help it burrow into the ground. The armadillo was adopted as Texas's official state small mammal in 1995.

Black-tailed Jackrabbits

Black-tailed jackrabbits are common throughout most of Texas, particularly in the state's grassy plains and arid scrublands. Also called desert hares, they have long hind legs and huge ears that let off excess heat.

Pronghorns

The pronghorn, found across western Texas, is the only horned animal that sheds its horns every year. It also is the fastest North American mammal. It can reach speeds of about 60 miles an hour.

Roadrunners

Roadrunners are found throughout the woodlands, grasslands, and deserts of Texas. They are long-legged birds that can run at a speed of more than 15 miles per hour. Although roadrunners are able to fly, they spend most of their time on the ground.

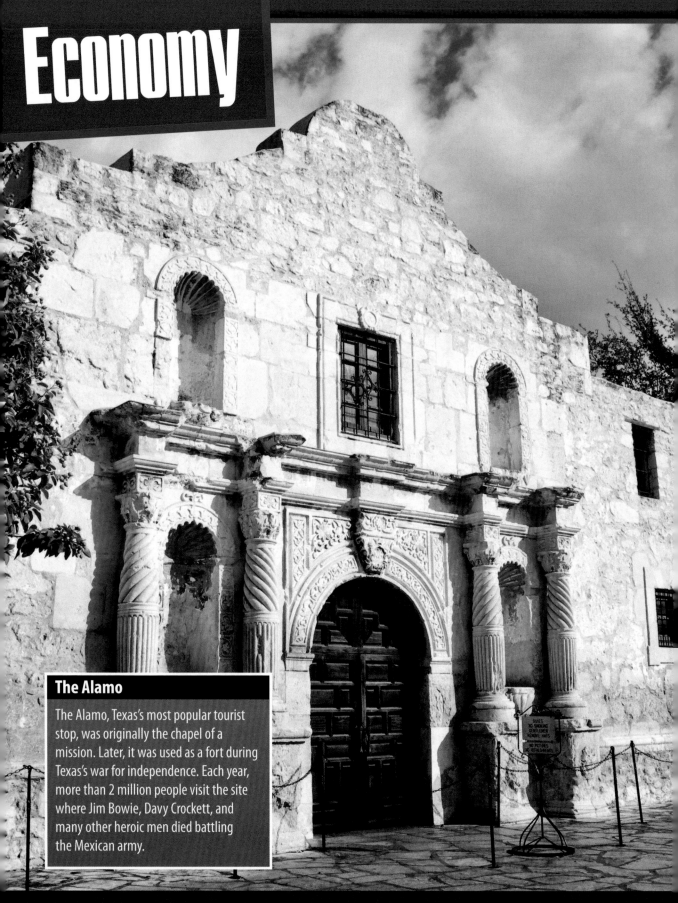

Economy

The Alamo

The Alamo, Texas's most popular tourist stop, was originally the chapel of a mission. Later, it was used as a fort during Texas's war for independence. Each year, more than 2 million people visit the site where Jim Bowie, Davy Crockett, and many other heroic men died battling the Mexican army.

Tourism

About 190 million U.S. travelers made trips to Texas destinations in 2009. The tourism sector of the state's economy earned more than $50 billion that year. Many people come to visit natural areas such as Big Bend National Park and Guadalupe Mountains National Park. The Gulf Coast has many beaches and **resorts**.

San Antonio is the state's top tourist destination. It is the gateway to the Alamo, site of a bloody battle during Texas's fight for independence from Mexico. Another major attraction is the city's River Walk, a tree-lined path with restaurants, shops, and boat docks along the San Antonio River. Every spring, thousands of music fans gather in Austin for the South by Southwest music festival. Six Flags Over Texas, near Dallas, is a popular amusement park with a historical theme.

Space Center Houston

This facility is the visitor center of NASA's Lyndon B. Johnson Space Center, the complex where human spaceflight training and monitoring take place. The attraction offers astronaut-related exhibits, theaters, and tours of the grounds.

Guadalupe Mountains National Park

Guadalupe Mountains National Park, located in west Texas, has four of the highest peaks in the state and more than 80 miles of hiking and walking trails. In addition to the rocky peaks, the park features desert landscapes and canyons.

Galveston Island

Galveston Island, in south Texas, is a Gulf Coast resort that offers 32 miles of beaches. Visitors there can also enjoy a variety of restaurants, art galleries, and antique shops.

Although Texas's economy has grown to include other industries, oil production is the state's largest source of income. This means that fluctuations in oil prices have a strong impact on the Texas economy.

Primary Industries

Since the first Texas oil boom in 1901, the oil and natural gas industry has played an important role in the state's economy. The mining, processing, and shipping of oil and natural gas are valuable sources of income in Texas. These products are sent through pipelines, in tanker trucks, and on ships to the rest of the country and the world.

Factories in Texas manufacture foods such as baked goods, soft drinks, and meat products. Technology companies build computers and other electronic equipment. Textiles, cars, trucks, and heavy equipment are also manufactured in the state. About one out of every six non-farm workers in Texas has a job in mining, logging, manufacturing, or construction.

Texas is among the top agricultural states in the U.S. More than three-fourths of its land is used for farming or grazing. In dry areas, **irrigation** helps farmers grow crops such as cotton and grain.

More people work in the **mining, oil,** and **gas industries** in **Texas** than in any other state.

Texas leads all states in the production of **cotton** and cottonseed.

Value of Goods and Services (in Millions of Dollars)

The mining industry is a very significant part of the Texas economy. Can you name some of the important minerals that are mined in the state?

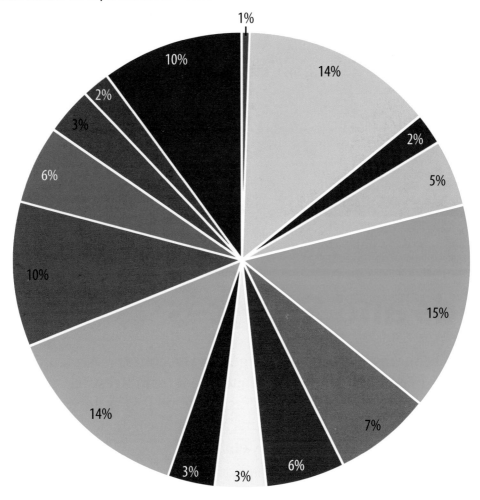

● Agriculture, Forestry, and Fishing	$11,176	● Information	$56,090
● Mining	$222,086	● Finance, Insurance, and Real Estate	$223,795
● Utilities	$36,687	● Professional and Business Services	$167,568
● Construction	$80,801	● Education, Health and Social Services	$93,599
● Manufacturing	$239,105	● Recreation and Accommodations	$52,513
● Wholesale Trade	$115,789	● Other Services	$32,986
● Retail Trade	$91,656	● Government	$161,456
● Transportation and Warehousing	$55,738		

Well-adapted to the southwest U.S. climate, the Angora goat has thrived in Texas. The state is the largest producer of mohair in the nation and third-largest in the world.

Goods and Services

The Texas economy is among the largest in the country. Agriculture has always been important to the state. Meat from livestock, grain, dairy products, apples, and pecans are just a few of Texas's agricultural products. With more than 245,000 farms and ranches, Texas has more farmland and pasture than any other state.

Besides pigs and cattle bred for meat, Texas is famous for its Angora goats, which produce the soft wool known as mohair. The state fruit, the red grapefruit, is grown in the lower Rio Grande area. Cotton and sorghum, which were once grown only in humid eastern Texas, are now major crops in the irrigated areas of the western plains. Rice, corn, and wheat are among the grains grown in the state.

The oil industry accounted for much of Texas's economy for many years. The importance of oil is still strong, but it has decreased with the introduction of other industries. These industries include food processing and aircraft manufacturing. Machinery and equipment production also bring a great deal of money into Texas.

Electronics are moneymakers as well. Texas Instruments is a major producer of electronic goods and military communications systems. Dell Computers, Apple Computers, and IBM also have large facilities in the state.

Chemicals are the leading manufactured goods in Texas. These include petroleum products. Other important chemical-based products include benzene, fertilizers, and sulfuric acid.

Texas has a growing technology industry. In 2014, the state surpassed California in technological exports.

Texas is the lead producer and refiner of oil in the United States.

Geronimo is a well-known leader of the Bedonkohe Apache who fought for Native American land rights.

The Caddo used the rich vegetation of their homeland to build grass houses, which often resembled beehives.

Native Americans

Early Native Americans in Texas were hunter-gatherers. They collected fruits and nuts and used stone tools to hunt. They mostly hunted large game, such as bison, also called buffalo. Later groups lived in settled villages and made pottery and tools. They built large ceremonial mounds that are still present today.

Two of the largest Native American groups that lived in the Texas area were the Caddo and the Jumano. The Caddo lived in farming villages near the Red River in northern and eastern Texas. They grew corn and vegetables and made homes out of grass and wood poles. The Jumano lived along the Rio Grande in the southwest. They farmed and traded with hunters from farther north. The Karankawa were **nomads** who roamed the Gulf Coast. They ate fish, small game, plants, and insects.

The Apache and Comanche roamed the plains on horseback and hunted bison. They ate the meat and used the rest of the animal to make shelters, blankets, clothing, and tools. These Native American groups also raided the settled farming villages of the region and often battled each other. By the 1700s, the Apache and Comanche were feared by Native Americans and European settlers alike.

Exploring the Land

The first explorers in Texas were Spaniards. In 1519, Alonso Álvarez de Pineda mapped out the Gulf of Mexico coast and likely went inland to what is now Texas. In 1528, Álvar Núñez Cabeza de Vaca's ship was wrecked near what is now Galveston. For years afterward, he and three other survivors wandered through the Texas region and the American Southwest. In 1536, they reached a Spanish settlement in Mexico. There, they told tales of cities full of gold and jewels that they had heard from the region's natives.

Timeline of Settlement

1598 Juan de Oñate claims all land surrounding the Rio Grande in the name of Spain's King Philip II.

Early Colonization

1685 French explorer René-Robert Cavelier, sieur de La Salle, establishes the Fort St. Louis colony and claims the Texas region for France.

1541 Francisco Vázquez de Coronado explores part of the Texas panhandle.

1687 La Salle is killed by his own men. Soon after, the remaining French colonists die or are killed by Native Americans.

1528 Álvar Núñez Cabeza de Vaca and his crew begin exploring Texas after being shipwrecked near Galveston.

1519 Spanish explorer Alonso Álvarez de Pineda maps the Texas coastline.

European Exploration

1700s Spain establishes Catholic missions throughout the Texas region.

In 1540, the explorer Francisco Vázquez de Coronado traveled from Mexico into the area that would become the southwest United States. He and his army found no sign of riches. In 1598, Juan de Oñate started exploring the area above the Rio Grande, looking for silver mines and hoping to spread Christianity. He began the establishment of missions and ranches along the upper Rio Grande. At this time, Spain had little interest in the rest of Texas.

French explorer René-Robert Cavelier, sieur de La Salle, created a colony in southeast Texas in 1685. He claimed the area for France and hoped to use it to fight the Spanish presence in Mexico. Within a few years, though, all French settlers at La Salle's colony had died from disease or had been killed. The Spanish decided to take over the land. Over the next century, they built missions throughout Texas. Many had military outposts nearby to protect colonists in conflicts with Native American groups.

1836 After a series of clashes, including the Alamo battle, the Republic of Texas is established.

1835 Texas colonists begin an armed revolt against Mexico.

1823 The Mexican government grants Stephen Austin a contract to bring 300 families from the United States into Texas, thereby establishing the first major colony.

Statehood and Civil War

1845 Texas is admitted to the Union as the 28th state.

1821 Mexico, including what is now Texas, gains independence from Spain.

1861–1865 Texas secedes from, or leaves, the Union and joins the Confederate States of America in 1861. The Civil War rages until 1865, when the Confederacy is defeated by the Union.

Independence From Spain, then Mexico

1870 Texas is readmitted to the Union as a state.

Spanish explorer Cabeza de Vaca's ship ran aground near Galveston, Texas, while searching for a mythical city of gold. It would take him and three other survivors eight years to find a Spanish settlement.

The First Settlers

In 1820, the Spanish gave a U.S. citizen named Moses Austin permission to start a colony in Texas, made up of settlers of European descent. However, he died in 1821 before he had the chance to recruit colonists for the planned settlement. In 1823, soon after Mexico won independence from Spain, Austin's son Stephen was given approval to bring about 300 families to the area.

The settlers moved to an area between the Colorado and Brazos rivers and called their colony San Felipe de Austin. The first few years were difficult. Crops failed, and the Karankawa people killed many settlers.

Over the next 15 years, 20,000 more settlers arrived, bringing 4,000 African slaves with them. Unhappy with the Mexican government, these settlers began fighting for independence in 1835. Much blood was shed in the war that followed. It was during this period that Texan forces were defeated at the famous battle of the Alamo. However, after the Texans won the Battle of San Jacinto on April 21, 1836, they succeeded in establishing the independent Republic of Texas. For the next nine years, Texas remained independent. It joined the United States on December 29, 1845.

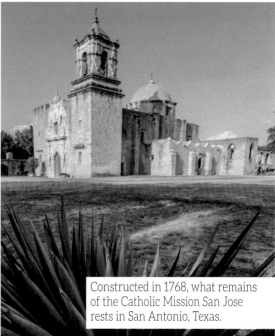

Constructed in 1768, what remains of the Catholic Mission San Jose rests in San Antonio, Texas.

Although the Battle of the Alamo was a loss for Texans, it inspired many to join the rebellion against Mexico. Texas defeated Mexico only a month later.

History Makers

The citizens of Texas have a reputation for their pioneering spirit, determination, bravery, and ingenuity. These qualities certainly are evident in some of the famous people who were born or lived in the state. From colonial leaders and politicians to military heroes and business people, Texans have left their mark on U.S. history.

Sam Houston (1793–1863)

Houston became a Tennessee congressman and governor during the 1820s, and then moved to Texas in the 1830s. He led rebel Texan forces to victory against the Mexican government, and he became the Republic of Texas's first president. Houston served as a U.S. senator from 1845 to 1859. He was elected governor of Texas in 1859 but resigned in protest two years later when the state joined the Confederacy.

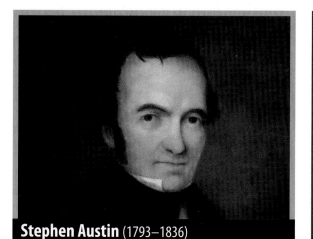

Stephen Austin (1793–1836)

Born in Virginia and raised in Missouri, Austin came to Texas in the 1820s. He sought to complete his late father's plan to establish a colony of settlers of European descent, in what was then a Mexican province. He helped establish laws for the colony and negotiated for the rights of the settlers. When Texas became an independent republic in 1836, Austin served as its first secretary of state.

Lyndon B. Johnson (1908–1973)

Johnson was the 36th president of the United States. Born near Stonewall, he eventually served as a Texas congressman and senator. In 1960, Johnson was elected U.S. vice president. He became president after John F. Kennedy's assassination in 1963. During his presidency, the country underwent many social reforms, but also was drawn deeper into the Vietnam War.

Barbara Jordan (1936–1996)

Born and raised in Houston, Jordan grew up to become the first African American woman from a southern state to be elected to the U.S. House of Representatives. Prior to her time in Congress, in the 1970s, she became the first African American woman to serve as a Texas state senator.

George W. Bush (1946–)

Bush, who was raised in Midland, served as Texas's governor before being elected the 43rd president of the United States in 2000. After the September 11, 2001, attacks, Bush led the country in a war against terrorism that included invasions of Iraq and Afghanistan. He is the son of the 41st U.S. president, George H. W. Bush.

Culture

There are more than 50,000 students enrolled at the University of Texas at Austin.

Houston, Texas is the largest city in the state by area and the fourth-largest in the nation. There are about 2.2 million people living in the city, not counting the greater metropolitan area.

The People Today

Texas has a highly diverse population. Many Texans are descended from people who came to the area from Mexico or from other parts of the United States. As of 2010, 12 percent of the population is African American. Thirty-two percent are Hispanic, and 73 percent are of European descent. Fifty-six percent of the state is married.

Counting the suburbs and smaller towns surrounding the central cities, Dallas–Fort Worth is the largest metropolitan area in the state, with more than 6.4 million people. Houston has about 5.9 million in its metropolitan area. The state also has hundreds of tiny towns.

About **88 percent** of Texans reside in **urban communities.**

Q Why would people choose to live in cities instead of more rural areas?

Built between 1882 and 1888, the Texas state capitol, in Austin, is the nation's sixth-tallest capitol building. It is taller than the United States Capitol in Washington, D.C.

State Government

Texas is governed under a constitution adopted in 1876. The government is divided into three sections. They are the legislative, executive, and judicial branches. The legislative branch includes the Senate and the House of Representatives, which make laws for Texas. There are 31 senators elected to four-year terms and 150 representatives elected to two-year terms. They decide on issues including how to spend state money.

The governor is head of the executive branch and is elected for a four-year term. The governor makes sure that laws are carried out. The judicial branch is made up of the courts. Most judges in Texas are elected to four-year terms. Texas has a very complex system of local, district, and state courts. The state's highest courts are the Supreme Court and the Court of Criminal Appeals.

Texas is divided into 254 counties. There are more than 1,000 cities and towns, each with its own local government. In the U.S. Congress, Texas has two seats in the Senate. The state originally had 32 seats in the U.S. House of Representatives. Due to population growth,that number was increased to 36 in 2013.

Before becoming governor of Texas in 2014, Greg Abbott served as the attorney general of Texas.

One of Texas's most famous military units, Terry's Texas Rangers, fought for the Confederacy in the American Civil War. A statue in front of the state capitol commemorates the unit.

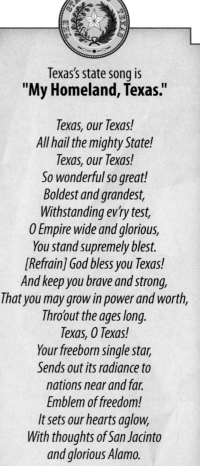

Texas's state song is
"My Homeland, Texas."

Texas, our Texas!
All hail the mighty State!
Texas, our Texas!
So wonderful so great!
Boldest and grandest,
Withstanding ev'ry test,
O Empire wide and glorious,
You stand supremely blest.
[Refrain] God bless you Texas!
And keep you brave and strong,
That you may grow in power and worth,
Thro'out the ages long.
Texas, O Texas!
Your freeborn single star,
Sends out its radiance to
nations near and far.
Emblem of freedom!
It sets our hearts aglow,
With thoughts of San Jacinto
and glorious Alamo.

* excerpted

Hispanic culture is celebrated in annual festivals and events throughout Texas.

Celebrating Culture

Many Hispanic Americans in the state are descended from people who lived in the area long before it became part of the United States. Others have come more recently from Mexico or other Latin American countries. Parades and festivals on Cinco de Mayo, May 5th, celebrate an 1862 Mexican military victory. Día de los Muertos, or Day of the Dead, is celebrated on November 1st and 2nd. It is a traditional Mexican holiday in which people remember their dead ancestors.

Hispanic music and food are very popular in Texas. People from around the country enjoy Tex-Mex **cuisine**. The food represents a blend of dishes traditionally eaten by the Native American and Hispanic people of south and west Texas. Cowboys have become central to Texas's cultural tradition. In the 1800s, cattle abounded on the open Texas range. Cowboys would round up the animals and drive them hundreds of miles to market or to railroads where they could be shipped east. Although the great cattle drives lasted for only a few years, this period left a lasting impression on Texas dress and culture.

Cowboy clothing originated on cattle ranches in northern Mexico. It was originally designed to make cattle work easier. Cowboy jeans lack **rivets** on the back pockets, which could damage saddles. Leather chaps protect legs from rain and brush. Wide hats protect the head from sun, rain, and blowing dust. Pointy boots slip smoothly into stirrups. Chuck-wagon foods, such as barbecued steak and beans, are an important part of Texas cooking. Rodeos help keep the skills of cowboy culture alive.

Chili has had a long history in Texas. The state's blend of cultures helped create Texas's favorite dish.

Each year, Texas hosts the Houston Livestock Show & Rodeo. It boasts the largest livestock exhibition and rodeo in the world.

Formed in Houston in 1969, blues rock band ZZ Top has been one of the United States' most beloved rock groups for more than 45 years.

Arts and Entertainment

Texas boasts several fascinating libraries and museums. The Texas State Library in Austin, established in 1839, is the state's oldest library. The Witte Museum in San Antonio has exhibits on the state's natural history, archaeology, and Native American art and culture. There are also paintings and artifacts from the days of early settlers. San Antonio is also home to the San Antonio Museum of Art, which houses paintings by U.S. artists, Greek and Roman antiquities, Asian art, and Native American, Mexican, and Spanish colonial art.

Texas has a rich musical heritage. Blues music developed from African American work songs and religious music after the Civil War. Country and western music is popular in Texas. Fiddles and guitars are often played in traditional country and western songs. The state also has produced many popular rock, R&B, and pop artists.

Due to the **dozens** of **music clubs** and **auditoriums** in Austin, the city calls itself **"the live music capital of the world."**

Jim Parsons, best known for his two-time Emmy Award-winning role as Sheldon Cooper on The *Big Bang Theory*, was born in Houston and studied theater at the University of Houston.

Another type of music in Texas is a blend of Mexican and German influences. This music is called *conjunto*, which is Spanish for "together," or Tex-Mex music. People from southeast Texas tap their toes to zydeco music, which originated with the Creoles of neighboring Louisiana.

Many famous authors have come from Texas. Katherine Anne Porter, born in the tiny town of Indian Creek, was a leading novelist and short-story writer. Her collected stories won the **Pulitzer Prize** in 1965. Larry McMurtry wrote dozens of books and screenplays before he won the Pulitzer for his novel *Lonesome Dove* in 1986.

Conjunto was born in late-nineteenth-century Texas, when German immigrants introduced the accordion to traditional Mexican musical styles.

Every October, the nation's largest state fair is held in Dallas. Country, blues, and rock musicians perform at the event. The venue also boasts the 212-foot Texas Star, the tallest Ferris wheel in the United States.

The State Fair of Texas takes place in Dallas every Fall. The fair has been promoting Texan agriculture and bringing Texans together since 1883.

Sports and Recreation

Texas has many professional sports teams. In Major League Baseball (MLB), the Houston Astros and the Texas Rangers play in the American League. The Rangers play their home games in Arlington, outside Dallas. The Dallas Cowboys have won the National Football League (NFL) championship five times. The Houston Texans brought professional football back to Houston in 2002, after the Oilers left the city in 1996.

The state is home to three teams in the National Basketball Association (NBA). They are the Dallas Mavericks, the Houston Rockets, and the San Antonio Spurs. Texas also claims the San Antonio Silver Stars, a team in the Women's National Basketball Association (WNBA).

The Dallas Cowboys are historically one of the NFL's best teams. They have been to eight Super Bowls and have won five.

Nolan Ryan, born in **Refugio** and raised in **Alvin**, threw a record **5,714 strikeouts** and **seven no-hitters** during his **27-year baseball career.**

Babe Didrikson Zaharias, a **Port Arthur native**, was one of the **best female golfers of all time.** She also **won two gold medals** in **track and field** at the **1932 Summer Olympics.**

One major professional hockey team calls Texas home. The Dallas Stars play in the National Hockey League (NHL). The team moved from Minnesota to Texas in 1993 and won the Stanley Cup in 1999.

College football is a popular sport in Texas. In addition, the state has its share of winning college football teams. The University of Texas, Texas Christian University, Southern Methodist University, and Texas A&M all have won National Collegiate Athletic Association (NCAA) championships over the years.

The Dallas Stars have sent five former players to the Hockey Hall of Fame.

Rodeo is an important sport in Texas throughout the year. Professional rodeo evolved in the 1800s from cowboy contests in roping and riding. Now, the best-known rodeo events are bull riding, bareback riding, and saddle bronco riding. In these events, a rider must stay on top of a bucking bull or horse for at least eight seconds while holding on with just one hand.

Steer wrestling pits a cowboy and a horse against a steer running alongside them. The cowboy must move from the horse to the steer and then wrestle the steer to the ground by turning its horns. Calf roping involves a rider lassoing a running calf with a rope. The cowboy then jumps off the horse and quickly ties up the calf's legs.

The San Antonio Spurs have won five NBA titles, most recently in 2014.

Get To Know
TEXAS

WESTERN DIAMONDBACK RATTLESNAKES ARE THE MOST WIDESPREAD VENOMOUS SNAKE FOUND IN TEXAS. THEY CAN GROW TO BE MORE THAN 7 FEET LONG.

The first word spoken from the **Moon** on July 20, 1969, was "**Houston.**" NASA's Mission Control is located in the city.

Wild camels once roamed the state. The last one was spotted in 1941 near Douglas, Texas.

The soft drink **Dr. Pepper** was **invented** by a **Waco pharmacist** in **1885.**

The first suspension bridge in the U.S. was the Waco Bridge, built in 1870.

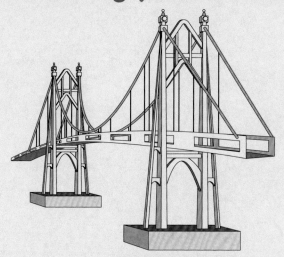

Chili is the **official** state dish of **Texas.**

In Clarendon, Texas, it is **illegal** to dust any public building with a *FEATHER DUSTER*.

Brain Teasers

What have you learned about Texas after reading this book? Test your knowledge by answering these questions. All of the information can be found in the text you just read. The answers are provided below for easy reference.

1 What is the capital of Texas?

2 Who first mapped out the Gulf of Mexico coast and likely went inland to what is now Texas?

3 Which country owned Texas before the U.S.?

4 On what date did Texas join the United States?

5 What Caddo word meaning "friends" or "allies" did the Spanish use to name the land of Texas?

6 In what year was the first Texas oil boom?

7 How many seats does Texas have in the House of Representatives as of 2013?

8 Who served as Texas's first secretary of state when Texas became an independent republic in 1836?

ANSWER KEY
1. Austin 2. Alonso Álvarez de Pineda 3. Mexico 4. December 29, 1845 5. Thecas 6. 1901 7. 36 8. Stephen Austin

Key Words

allies: people who are friendly with one another or who have made an agreement to work together

barren: lacking any useful plant life

commercial: sold for profit

conservation: preservation or protection of natural resources

cuisine: style of preparing food

irrigation: using ditches, streams, or pipes to bring water to dry land

nomads: people with no fixed home who move from one place to another looking for food

panhandle: a narrow strip of territory projecting from the main territory of one state into another state

ports: harbors where ships dock

Pulitzer Prize: any of a series of annual prizes awarded for outstanding achievement in U.S. journalism, letters, and music

republic: a country governed by an elected government

resorts: places people go to for relaxation and recreation

rivets: metal bolts or pins

stalactite: a tapering structure hanging like an icicle from the roof of a cave

Index

Alamo 20, 21, 29, 30, 31, 37
Austin 4, 8, 18, 21, 29, 30, 34, 36, 40, 46
Austin, Stephen 8, 29, 33, 46

Big Bend National Park 6, 11, 21
Bush, George W. 33

Cabeza de Vaca, Álvar Núñez 28, 30
Caddo Lake 11

El Capitan 10
El Paso 8

Galveston Island 21
Guadalupe Mountains 10, 21
Gulf of Mexico 6, 8, 12, 14, 28, 46

Hispanic Americans 5, 35, 38
Houston 21, 33, 35, 39, 40, 42, 44
Houston, Sam 32
Hueco Tanks State Historic Site 8

Johnson, Lyndon B. 21, 33
Jordan, Barbara 33

La Salle, René-Robert Cavelier, sieur de 28, 29

Mexico 5, 7, 8, 12, 14, 21, 28, 29, 30, 31, 35, 38, 39, 46

Native Americans 7, 26, 27, 28, 29, 38, 40
Natural Bridge Caverns 9

oil 5, 14, 22, 24, 25, 46

Padre Island 11

ranching 5, 7, 24, 29, 39
Republic of Texas 5, 8, 29, 30, 32
rodeos 5, 9, 39, 43

San Antonio 18, 21, 31, 40, 42, 43
Spain (Spanish) 5, 7, 28, 29, 30, 40, 41, 46
Stockyards National Historic District 9

Log on to www.av2books.com

AV[2] by Weigl brings you media enhanced books that support active learning. Go to www.av2books.com, and enter the special code found on page 2 of this book. You will gain access to enriched and enhanced content that supplements and complements this book. Content includes video, audio, weblinks, quizzes, a slide show, and activities.

AV[2] Online Navigation

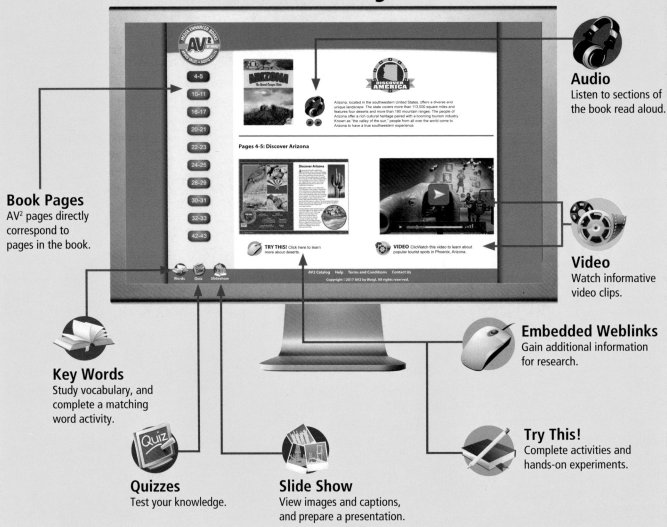

Book Pages
AV[2] pages directly correspond to pages in the book.

Audio
Listen to sections of the book read aloud.

Video
Watch informative video clips.

Key Words
Study vocabulary, and complete a matching word activity.

Embedded Weblinks
Gain additional information for research.

Quizzes
Test your knowledge.

Slide Show
View images and captions, and prepare a presentation.

Try This!
Complete activities and hands-on experiments.

AV[2] was built to bridge the gap between print and digital. We encourage you to tell us what you like and what you want to see in the future.

Sign up to be an AV[2] Ambassador at www.av2books.com/ambassador.

Due to the dynamic nature of the Internet, some of the URLs and activities provided as part of AV[2] by Weigl may have changed or ceased to exist. AV[2] by Weigl accepts no responsibility for any such changes. All media enhanced books are regularly monitored to update addresses and sites in a timely manner. Contact AV[2] by Weigl at 1-866-649-3445 or av2books@weigl.com with any questions, comments, or feedback.